"Master Yin Shi Zi's book so enthralled me that I read it in a single sitting. His training in classical Chinese medicine and as a professor of physiology enables him to express both his own experiences and his guide to cultivating a practice of these methods in a language easily comprehensible to the modern reader. His book is a wonderful contribution to our understanding of the nature of Taoist/Buddhist yoga, meditation, and inner science."

—*Glenn H. Mullin, author of* Selected Works of the Dalai Lama *and* Death and Dying

"The reader can really better understand the mental and physical phenomena encountered when progressing through meditation. If anyone ever wondered what changes may occur during intense study of meditation, this book helps to provide answers."

—*Master Tsung Hwa Jou, author of* The Dao of Taijiquan *and* The Tao of Meditation

"This wonderful book has been very influential in my own practice and I was elated to find that Shifu Hwang and Cheney Crow have completed such a clear translation. *Tranquil Sitting* provides inspiration for all those who want to practice meditation, but may feel that their life contradicts or obstructs that practice. Yin Shi Zi is deservedly considered one of China's most celebrated meditation practitioners."

—*Stuart Alve Olson, author of* Cultivating the Ch'i

YIN SHI ZI

TRANSLATED BY
SHIFU HWANG AND CHENEY CROW, PH.D.

Forewords by Master Zhongxian Wu and Glenn H. Mullin

Tranquil Sitting

A TAOIST JOURNAL ON MEDITATION
AND CHINESE MEDICAL QIGONG

YIN SHI ZI

SINGING
DRAGON

LONDON AND PHILADELPHIA

This edition published in 2013
by Singing Dragon
an imprint of Jessica Kingsley Publishers
116 Pentonville Road
London N1 9JB, UK
and
400 Market Street, Suite 400
Philadelphia, PA 19106, USA

www.singingdragon.com

First published in 1994
by Dragon Door Publications

Library of Congress Cataloging in Publication Data
A CIP catalog record for this book is available from the Library of Congress

British Library Cataloguing in Publication Data
A CIP catalogue record for this book is available from the British Library

ISBN 978 1 84819 112 9
eISBN 978 0 85701 090 2

Printed and bound in Great Britain

MEDITATION DEVELOPS YOUR innate energies. With practice, you can take charge of your mind and body, preventing disease before it arises. Shouldn't everyone make an effort to learn something like this? Superficially, meditation looks easy, but if you practice without patience, determination, and a long-term sense of devotion you will never realize its benefits. To give readers a guide to meditation, I have therefore summarized my many decades of experience.

Yin Shi Zi
October, 1954

CONTENTS

A Taoist Journal on Meditation and Chinese Medical Qigong by Yin Shi Zi

Foreword

SIMPLICITY IS THE BEST

The Dao 道 is simple.
The healing method that follows the Dao is
simple.
A harmonious life is simple.
Qigong 氣功 is a way of life and a way to help
people live simply in health and happiness.

IN MY AUDIO CD, *Three Treasures—The Medicines of Shamanic Healing and Internal Alchemy*, published by Chinese Wisdom Traditions, I emphasize that there is only one type of disease: Qi stagnation (or blockage). The *NeiJing* 內經 (one of the most important classical texts of traditional Chinese medicine) mentions this idea—*BuTongZeTong* 不通則痛—"Where there is obstruction, there is pain." This obstruction forms irregular patterns in the body on either energetic or physical planes. Left unchecked, these areas of stagnation are then later diagnosed as the myriad of diseases known to modern medicine. The *NeiJing* further states that all pain is related to the Heart. The Heart in this context refers to the mind and to our Shen 神, the spirit within our body. In other words, the classics tell us that an uneasy mind or a weak spiritual body will cause a weakness in the physical body. This connection should never be ignored.

By learning to work with Heart and Qi within the body, one may recover from illness, restore health, and maintain wellbeing. In *Tranquil Sitting*, the remarkable Qigong master JiangWeiQiao 蔣維喬 (CE 1873–1958) teaches us some simple traditional Chinese sitting meditation methods to work with our Heart and Qi. He personally recovered from tuberculosis and other significant health issues through his dedicated cultivation practice. These simple methods originate from Daoist internal alchemy meditation and the TianTai 天台 school meditation techniques. The TianTai school is one of the Eight Buddhist Schools in China. The founder master, ZhiYi 智顗 (CE 538–597), created the TianTai school based on his knowledge of Buddhism, Daoism, and Confucianism.

In 1914, JiangWeiQiao introduced these ancient meditation methods to the general public through his book *YinShiZi JingZuoFa* 因是子靜坐瀘 (*YinShiZi's Tranquil Sitting Methods*. In *Tranquil Sitting*, this title is translated by Shifu Hwang and Cheney Crow as *Yin Shi Zi's Meditation*), which was published under his spiritual name YinShiZi 因是子. To my knowledge, this marked the first time these ancient methods were explained in modern language, without any mention of traditional internal cultivation terms such as YinYang, Five Elements, KanLi (water and fire), or Lead and Mercury, making the content very accessible to the general public. While JiangWeiQiao focused on the practical aspects of traditional meditation techniques, he also included stories of his personal insights in order to give his audience an idea of the long-term process involved in achieving deep healing results.

Over the years, his book has been very well received throughout China, having been republished over twenty times, and is widely considered to be a modern classic Qigong self-healing book. There are countless individuals who have recovered from all manner of illness and disease by studying and practicing methods from his book. In honor of his great contribution to our people and to our culture, all throughout China we regard him as the Grand Father of modern Qigong.

I am so pleased that Singing Dragon is republishing the English version of Master Jiang's tranquil sitting methods. It is my honor to write this foreword and help re-introduce his exceptional work to the Western world. If you are looking for some simple methods to help you recover from illness, and live in health and peace, I believe that with devotion to your daily practice, this marvelous book will help you achieve your dreams.

Harmonious Qi,

ZhongXian Wu

Summer Solstice, 2012
Orchard House, Blue Ridge Mountains

Foreword

In 1954, at the age of eighty-one, the venerable Chinese master Yin Shi Zi put to paper a remarkable account of his experiences in the practice of meditation, in which he had combined Taoist and Buddhist techniques in a traditional blend of spiritual exercises for health and enlightenment. Moreover, he complemented his spiritual biography with a section on practical exercises for inducing the experiences of body and mind that he himself had realized.

From its most ancient times China developed and preserved a most unique culture of meditation for health, harmony, and self-fulfillment. The early Taoist masters well understood the nature of the human predicament, and responded by setting forth clear guidelines whereby trainees could extract the essence of the human potential. Later, with the importation of Buddhism from India, these two traditions confronted one another in what may be called a most exquisite marriage of spiritual technologies. Master Yin Shi Zi addresses this marriage not as historical data, but as a living dynamic. He began his training as a Taoist, and later supplemented his practice with elements from the Tian Tai school of Chinese Buddhism. Several decades later he complemented this body of techniques with several methods coming from the esoteric Vajrayana

Buddhism of Tibet. He discusses these with disarming intimacy and humility.

From birth Master Yin Shi Zi was afflicted by chronic health problems, and as a teenager took up the practice of Taoist yoga and meditation solely in order to cure himself. Only after he had witnessed the healing powers of these techniques did he become fascinated with the spiritual implications of the methods he had been utilizing, and thus begin to apply himself to them from within a spiritual perspective. His account of his experiences in these two areas, firstly medical and then spiritual, thus provides the reader with a glimpse of the multidimensional impact of these ancient practices.

His training in classical Chinese medicine and as a professor of physiology enables him to express both his own experiences and his guide to cultivating a practice of these methods in a language easily comprehensible to the modern reader. He lived in a special period, when China was making the transition from an ancient and somewhat insular culture to a modern nation aware of international attitudes and perspectives. Thus he stood on a bridge in Chinese history, and his education on both sides of the bridge provided him with a unique insight. His book is a wonderful contribution to our understanding of the nature of Taoist/Buddhist yoga, meditation, and inner science.

Shifu Hwang and Cheney Crow have done an excellent job of translating the manuscript from the original Chinese, and we owe a great debt to them for their efforts.

Glenn H. Mullin

Author and lecturer
October, 1994

ABOUT THE TRANSLATION

Y IN SHI ZI's book, written in 1954, was published in a collection of writings on meditation called *Jing Zuo Fa Ji Yao* (*The Collection of the Way of Meditation*), by His Yo Publications in January 1962. Yin Shi Zi, once a professor of physiology at Kuan Hua University, divided his text into two sections. The first is didactic, with sections on theory, physiology, preparation, and instruction for meditation. The second section is a diary account of his personal experience and meditation practice (his illness, his early Taoist practice, his self-healing, then his initiation into and practice of the Tibetan Tantric practice of opening the crown of the head).

Translators make many choices as they work. We chose to adhere as closely as possible to a literal translation, which the differences between Chinese and English render almost impossible. There are instances, therefore, where we added words or phrases [in square brackets] to the original Chinese to facilitate reading. All parentheses are from the original text. Transcription for Chinese characters was done using the Chinese government's Latin-Han Zi transcription system, which is promoted by the Confucius School.

It is with humble gratitude that we offer this unrevised text to fellow seekers, in hopes they may experience what we did in working on this somewhat awkward text: moments of inspiration, wonder, reassurance, and a heightened sense of compassion for those on the path we share.

Cheney Crow, Ph.D.

February, 2012

TRANSLATOR'S INTRODUCTION

My life was profoundly influenced by this book, originally titled *Jing Zuo Fa* and written by Master Jiang Wei Chiao, who took the Taoist name Yin Shi Zi. The guidance it offers helped lead me out of an unhealthy life towards a life devoted to cultivation of the Tao. My friend and student Cheney Crow agreed to collaborate with me to translate this book into English. We completed this work in November, 1993, and it was first published in 1994. We are pleased that Singing Dragon has chosen to make this book available to others interested in learning these methods and reading about the experiences of Yin Shi Zi as he began and developed his practice.

Like him, I was unhealthy in body and spirit before I began meditation. For ten years after graduating from university in Taiwan, I ran a business. Like many other businessmen, I indulged in smoking, drinking, nightlife. Because of my unrestricted lifestyle, my health and my business deteriorated. I developed a persistent cough. When my business began to fail, I was coughing up blood. In 1982 I was bankrupt, very sad in heart, and physically exhausted. I emigrated to the United States.

Recognizing my undisciplined lifestyle as the root cause of my physical and financial distress, I sought help. To heal my body and my mind, I chose Taoism. I studied many Taoist scriptures, but they were hard to understand, and even harder to practice. Eventually, I found this book. I could understand the author's writing and his instructions, so I followed its principles and began to practice meditation.

At first, I was troubled by the meditation postures and by random thoughts; however, I persevered. After almost four months, I began to notice physical effects from the practice, and changes in my body. I felt a pulsing force in three areas of my back: at my tailbone (Wei Lu), middle spine (Jia Ji), and at the base of my head (Yu Zhen). I had the sensation of sweet dew flowing down from the crown of my head, across my face, down through my chest to the lower Dan Tien (about 4 inches below the navel). Three times I had a sensation, and intuitive awareness, of white light shooting out from my chest. When this happened, I know I had completed the Xiao Zho Tian (small heaven circulation) training.

My body and my mind were healing; I felt healthy and optimistic. My memory became clearer. There were other physical sensations. I heard a sound like wind blowing in my ears, sometimes all day. I felt a buzz, like electricity, at the crown of my head. There was so much movement in my back that it felt like I was getting a massage. I did not feel tired, even when I worked two or more hours longer than usual.

I knew then that Taoism was not empty talk, that there were true benefits in this lifetime. I studied more Taoism scriptures. One day, as I read a book by master Chang San Feng, these words got my attention, "Training in Tai Chi is the way to build a foundation for entering the Tao." I began diligent study and practice of Tai Chi and other martial arts. I became proficient, and was a martial arts instructor for twenty years, teaching Tai Chi, Kung Fu, self-defense, and wrestling.

The goal of the Taoist practitioner is to become immortal. The average life span, called Yi Jia Zi (one circle) is about sixty years. With complete Taoist meditation training, a practitioner can live longer. Complete Taoist meditation training should include: Xiao Zho Tian (small heaven circulation), Da Zho Tian (large heaven circulation), and Dao He Che (reverse heaven circulation). The secret of Taoist meditation is to manipulate the Zhong Qi (ancestor Qi). The Zhong Qi is stored in the inner chest, in muscle fiber enclosing the internal organs, and in the organs themselves. Zhong Qi can nourish the internal organs, but if it cannot travel and circulate through to the crown of the head, and the four limbs, the human body slowly declines. Taoist meditation training releases the Zhong Qi into the twelve regular meridians and the six extraordinary meridians. This circulation will improve the practioner's health, and naturally his life span will increase. If he lives respecting a healthy lifestyle and Taoist principles, he can live to be one hundred and twenty years. Then he can be called immortal.

Master Jiang Wei Chiao (Yin Shi Zi) studied Xiao Zho Tian (small heaven circulation), which I also studied and practice. This is a Taoist art. He also studied two Buddhist arts, Zhi Kwen Fa (resting mind by visualization) and the Tantric art, Po Wa (breaking the tile, breaking the crown), which he describes in this book. Although he studied and used Buddhist practices, and did not have the opportunity to receive a complete Taoist training, he chose and adopted a Taoist name, Yin Shi Zi. With his Taoist name he wrote this very valuable writing, which is of great benefit to others. I experienced this myself, as I have explained.

This book helped me begin my Taoist practice. For thirty years I have studied and practiced Taoism. It has changed my mind and my body. I have chosen a Taoist name. This book helped me begin.

Shifu Hwang

The Taoist Bronze
in Bastrop, Texas
April, 2012

A TAOIST JOURNAL

On Meditation and Chinese Medical Qigong

BY YIN SHI ZI

PREFACE

CHINESE TRADITIONAL MEDICINE is noteworthy for its preventive benefits. I wanted to write a book that would show how Taoist meditation integrates into this system. Many ancient scriptures describe meditation in both preventive and curative terms, but most of them are written in terminology deriving from concepts not easily understood by the lay reader: terms relating to Yin and Yang, the Five Elements, K'an and Li, from the I Ching, or Lead and Mercury, from internal alchemy. Also, the theories behind these scriptures contained secrets which could not be shared with all, so they could not be widely disseminated.

Many years ago I wished to write an easily understood book and present it to the world, but, having little time, I postponed this wish until 1914, when I was forty-one years old, and saw a Japanese method, Okada-Torajiro meditation, named after the man who created it. After this time I could no longer remain silent, so I wrote a book called *Yin Shi Zi's Meditation*. "Meditation" in Chinese means "tranquil sitting," and has been practiced for several centuries. During the Sung dynasty, Confucian scholars used meditation to regulate their conduct. During the Ming dynasty, Yuan Liao Fan wrote a book called *The Secret of Tranquil Sitting* and in it presented a method resembling the precepts of tranquility found in the Zen school of Buddhism. Since the phrase "tranquil sitting" is easily understood and remembered, I have also chosen it to be the title of my book. Human beings have four basic postures: walking, sitting, lying down, and relaxing. Of these four, only the sitting posture can make the whole body calm down and enter into the state of tranquility, so both the Taoists and the Buddhists chose this posture for meditation. Although it is true that the postures of lying down and walking can also be used for meditation, the practitioner will find that using these postures is more difficult than sitting.

My first publication sold many copies. In 1918, when I was forty-five years old, I wrote another book called *The Continuation of Yin Shi Zi's Meditation*, in which I interpreted my experiences based on the teachings of Zhi Kuan's principles of the Tian Tai sect of Buddhism. These two books sold very fast and have been reprinted several dozen times. Now thirty-six years have elapsed, and I am eighty-one years old. I have accumulated more experience, and witnessed the existence of Extraordinary Acupoints and the related eight meridians, which I would like to submit as a reference for medical care. This book presents more material than the previous two books on the theory, method, and experience of tranquil sitting.

PART I

Yin Shi Zi sitting in meditation

CHAPTER ONE

The Theory of Tranquil Sitting

The meaning of tranquility

Our earth rotates continuously. Compared with the size of the earth, human beings seem almost ant-like, yet we cannot sense the earth's movement at all. We are ceaselessly active. Even when we sleep, our heartbeat never stops. Our universe is full of constant activity, without a moment's stillness. For this reason, I say that the terms "stillness" and "activity" exist only as relative concepts. When the activity of our bodies and our minds is out of sync with the rhythm of the earth's activity, we call both "action." When we don't act and our state synchronizes with the rhythm of the earth's activity, we call this stillness.

After a person has worked for some time, he has to rest. After working for several hours, a factory worker must have time to rest. In schools, teachers strain their brains during a fifty minute class and have ten minutes afterwards to rest. This rest is a state of stillness. However, this state of stillness may not be complete physically and mentally. Sometimes the body is resting, but the mind remains active, and we cannot sense the true meaning of stillness.

The conflicting states of the body and the mind

The mind and body are always in conflict. Until we become aware of this conflict, we cannot sense it. For example, if a person behaves badly, he will face a struggle with his conscience, whether he is good or ill-natured. Prompted by his desires, a person behaves badly and later regrets his behavior. This is the conflict between the mind and the body. The ancients called this "the struggle between conscience and desire." A man who can use his conscience to subdue his desire is called a good man. When his conscience overpowers his desire, this conflict is resolved.

Why is there so much conflict? Because no element in the universe exists without another, conflicting element, which is its complement. When each element is confronted with its complement, the two become opposites. The directions are East, West, South, and North. The sizes are small and large, high and low, long and short. Shapes are round and square. Time is ancient or modern, going or coming, morning or evening, winter or summer. Men's affairs bring happiness or calamity, joy or anger, love or hatred, righteousness or sinfulness, kindness or evil. Witnessing these polarities, we know that each of our activities will eventually produce its opposite. Activity brings contradiction into being. A man who has a high level of cultivation has a placid and quiet mind. He does not allow the self to exist, and thus achieves selflessness. When he meets with conflicting situations, he can rely on his consciousness to guide him and so reconcile the conflict. Tranquil sitting is the practice that allows this process to be effective.

CHAPTER TWO

The Physiological Features of Meditation

The relationship between tranquil sitting and normal physical function

Tranquil sitting can influence the entire physical body, including the arms and legs externally and the organs internally. No part of the body remains unaffected by meditation. I do not, however, intend to give a discourse on physiology, so I won't give detailed illustrations of these effects. I will just try to give a general description of the nervous, circulatory, respiratory, and regenerative systems.

In the past, people preferred to regard mind and body as two separate entities. Recently, though, the physiologist Pavlov discovered that the cerebral cortex dominates both the external and internal aspects of the body's equilibrium, and generates all of its reflexes. We can therefore affirm now that the human spirit and physical body are not two different things and cannot be separated—they are a unified system.

There are both conditioned and non-conditioned reflexes. Non-conditioned reflexes are innate, instinctive rather than learned behavior, and are the simpler type of reflex. For example, the eyes close abruptly upon contact with an object. The nose sniffs in reaction to the stimulus of a smell. The throat coughs or vomits upon contact with an unpleasant stimulus. The hands withdraw abruptly upon contact with a hot object. All these are non-conditioned reflexes.

There are never enough such reflexes to deal with the changing environment of daily life. However, when similar non-conditioned reflexes accumulate sufficiently, the cerebral cortex is able to link them and transform these into a conditioned reflex. For example, the plum has a sour flavor; eat a plum, and the mouth waters. This is a non-conditioned reflex. Later, you can see a plum and, without putting it into your mouth, produce saliva, quenching your thirst. What was previously unconditioned has become conditioned. Through such association and reaction, which may cause physical transformation, people can free themselves from the restrictions of unconditioned reactions by consciously guiding them into conditioned reactions.

Just as our thoughts may be replicated in written and verbal language, a second type of stimulus signal can be generated by our thoughts, to replicate the first type of signals, those produced by real physical stimulation. By practicing this method, the limits of the conditioned reflex are eliminated. Physical reflexes have two features: excitation and suppression. When a nerve is stimulated, the entire body, as well as the site of the stimulus, will be excited by the brain. When the excitation reaches a certain threshold, this reaction will be suppressed by the brain.

What has tranquil sitting to do with the nervous system? When the brain simply reacts to stimuli, this state may be called, in religious terms, random thinking. When random thinking arises, or diminishes, there is not a moment's stability. This can disturb the mind, making it uneasy, and furthermore it can influence the health of the physical body.

When someone is caught in the middle of a secretive act, he will blush. If a person meets with a sudden shock, his face will appear greenish white. This indicates that emotional reactions influence the activity of the blood vessels. When you feel ashamed, your arteries expand; if you feel shock or a sudden surprise, your veins expand. If you feel happy, you will have a good appetite. If you feel sad, you can look at food, but cannot bring yourself to eat it. This indicates that emotional reactions can also influence the function of the stomach and the digestive system.

There are many such illustrations, which indicate that our spirit should be calmed down, so that the function of our reflexes will return to normal. The autonomic nervous system, which includes the sympathetic nervous system and the sub-sympathetic nervous system can maintain balance, so that our bodies and minds may remain in harmony. However, random thinking is difficult to control. A practitioner could devote himself to meditation and continue practicing for a long time before his entire body could be unified, and he would be able to control all parts of his body. The ancients say that when you can sit tranquilly your power over the body is like that of a king surrounded by a hundred subjects who await your command. So we can see the close relationship between meditation and the central nervous system.

The circulatory system

Blood is an element fundamental to human life, for it circulates throughout the body without a moment's pause. The circulatory system includes two main parts, the heart and the blood vessels. The heart is the central device, pumping out red blood through the arteries to the whole body as it simultaneously receives the veins' purple blood. Blood vessels are channels for transferring blood to all parts of the body. One type of channel is called an artery. The vein, another type of channel, returns blood to the heart. The task of the circulatory system is to maintain the blood's balance in the body so that the activity of each part of the body can meet the requirements of the whole body and develop. In this process, each of the circulatory system's tasks may be modified relative to the activity of the whole body. When a specific part of the body is especially active, blood circulation in this area will intensify, so more blood accumulates. For example, when you are full of food, the blood in the stomach will circulate more intensely. After exercising, the limbs will feel full because of the rapidly circulating blood. The opposite is also true; inactive limbs will feel the shortage of circulation. Thus, at all times, every part of a healthy body will receive an appropriate amount of blood, neither too much nor too little. The circulatory system can function normally.

The circulation of the blood and the body's continuous functioning do not depend solely on the expansion and contraction of the heart and blood vessels. The functions also rely on a generalized organization which regulates the entire system. It is the central nervous system which governs these activities, primarily the cerebral cortex. Pavlov said that the nerves of the blood vessels which connect the brain and spine to the heart have two functions: excitation and suppression.

The first of these, excitation, will quicken the heartbeat, contracting the diameter of the blood vessels. The latter will weaken and slow down the heartbeat, and make the blood vessels dilate. These two functions are reciprocal, and are intrinsically related, for the adjustment of the activity of the circulatory system.

When the circulatory system is inactive, a person becomes ill. Both Chinese and Western doctors check the pulse for diagnosis. Whenever the circulatory system is sluggish, there must be either an internal or external cause.

The internal causes:

Though the internal organs are in the domain of the central nervous system, they still take orders from the spinal nervous system and the autonomic nervous system (sympathetic and sub-sympathetic systems), which connect indirectly with the brain. The onset of a disease causes the internal organs to have an abnormal reflex, and the flow of blood will become unstable.

A person's blood is mostly preserved in an area of the stomach where its muscles are powerless. Sometimes the muscles cannot expel the blood entirely, so the blood becomes stale. This condition leads to insufficient blood in some other part of the body.

Since we cannot directly influence the activity of the internal organs, we cannot sense when the blood becomes sluggish. Even if we are aware of this situation, we can do nothing but wait until the disease occurs, and then consult a doctor.

The arteries' blood begins close to the heart, therefore it is powerful. The veins' blood starts from the region of the head and the four limbs and then returns to the heart. It remains comparatively far from the heartbeat, so its power is much weaker, which is why the veins' blood can easily be retained in the abdominal area.

The external causes:

Obvious effects are the seasonal changes from summer to winter, the flu, and external wounds of physical and chemical origin, all of which make the circulatory system lose functional properties.

When you maintain a practice in which you focus on the abdomen as your center of gravity, your abdominal muscles will, after much practice, become powerful and flexible. You will be able to expel stale blood from the abdominal area, and let it return to the heart. You will also feel stronger sensations from the internal organs. If an internal organ functions improperly, you will be able to sense this situation earlier, and through meditation restore the circulatory system to perfect condition. You will not easily contract an illness. Practicing this preventive medical care is much better than contracting an illness and then consulting a doctor for a cure.

Breathing

Breathing plays an essential role in supporting human life. Everyone realizes the importance of eating to maintain life. If you stop eating, you will suffer hunger and thirst, and eventually die. However, breathing is more important than eating. If a man fasts for seven days he could die, but if his mouth and nose are covered and he doesn't breathe, he cannot survive longer than half an hour. This illustrates that breathing is more important than food. You need to exchange money for food, and acquiring money depends on your wages. For breathing, you can obtain air freely from the atmosphere, a process which requires neither money nor labor. That is the reason ordinary people realize the importance of food, but do not realize the importance of breathing.

Energy and calories are necessary to human bodily functions, and are derived primarily from the oxygenation of foods. The stomach is like a steam engine. Digestion of food is just like the burning of a steam engine. In terms of physics, this burning requires oxygen and produces carbon dioxide. In the process of oxygenation, oxygen and carbon dioxide, which came from our atmosphere, return to it. This is an exchange of internal and external bodies, as is breathing. When oxygen is inhaled, it reaches the lungs, then the heart. It makes the blood travel from the veins to the arteries, and, through the arteries, the blood travels to other parts of the body. Then it leaves the blood vessels and begins its restorative role in cell production, during which the cells will generate carbon dioxide, a poison which must be expelled from the body. The carbon dioxide then retraces this route in reverse, from the veins to the heart, from the heart to the lungs, and finally to the mouth and nose, where it is exhaled.

The air entering or exiting the lungs depends mainly on the activity of the chest muscles and the diaphragm. This is the activity of breathing, which functions incessantly day and night (in actuality, there is an almost imperceptible pause in breathing and in the heartbeat), so that you can keep your inhalation and exhalation in balance. Breathing is governed entirely by the central nervous system.

When we breathe in, the air is taken in through the nostrils and throat, to the trachea, the bronchia, and into the lungs. When we breathe out, the air in the alveoles follows the original route to exit. The lungs are divided into left and the right. The left lung has two lobes. The right lung has three lobes. Physiologists estimate that man's lungs have a total of seventy-five billion alveoles, which, spread out, would cover an area of about seventy square meters. About fifty-five square meters are involved in the functions of breathing. Relatively speaking, this space is thirty times larger than the surface area of the human body. We cannot imagine that such a small chest could contain so much. This illustrates to us how elaborate the construction of the lung is.

Though breathing may sometimes involve nitrogen and water vapor, these are not essential substances. Inhaling is primarily ingestion of oxygen. Exhaling is expulsion of carbon dioxide. This process is necessary to make the purple color of blood in the veins change to a red color before it flows into the arteries. Hence the circulation of the blood is totally dependent on the assistance of breathing. In continuous circulation, the blood makes a circuit through the entire body every twenty-four seconds, which results in thirty-six hundred circuits in a twenty-four-hour period. The breathing of a human being may reach twenty thousand repetitions in a day, an intake of approximately three hundred and eighty cubic meters of fresh air.

If we estimate that the volume of blood in every person's body is two and a half liters, then nine thousand kilograms of blood are purified daily. It is difficult to believe that people cannot sense this remarkable event.

The combination of one inhalation and one exhalation is called a single breath. People's lives depend on this breath. If you cannot catch your breath in time, you will suffocate and die. The practice of meditation addresses this problem, which is a fundamental requirement of life. All Buddhist and Taoist priests and health instructors emphasize the practice of breathing. The initial step is to teach breathing techniques, and even when you attain a high level this practice is continued.

Regeneration

Regeneration is a common characteristic of all living things, the signature of life's activity, the demarcation between living and non-living beings. Regeneration is a basic physiological activity of a highly evolved being. The structure of the human body has attained a very high level of complexity. It requires nutrition and oxygen for its regeneration, a process which involves a sequence of very complicated functions.

Waste byproducts from the regenerative process also undergo a very elaborate process before being eliminated from the body. Waste substances produced by the human being are solid, liquid, and gas. The solid and liquid wastes can be eliminated as stool, urine, and perspiration. Gas can be expelled through the lungs and the mouth or nose. Among these, the procedure of expelling gas is the most important for good health. Circulation and breathing, whose functions are assured by the central nervous system which regulates all bodily events, are also auxiliary activities of regeneration.

The regenerative process has two parts. One is constructive regeneration, which includes our body's development, replenishment, the restoration of energy, and nutrition. A growing child has not completed his development; his constructive growth is still in progress. An adult has reached his full development, so replenishment is his body's main task. Another type of regeneration involves the process of breaking things down, whether it be of tissue, energy, or food. Any such process can produce energy and calories. After energy is produced, part of it can be used to maintain body temperature, and the excess parts are quickly released from the body. In other words, the procedure of regeneration includes two continuous and inseparable steps.

The first of these steps is the compounding and the breaking down of tissue or food. The second step is the production, use, and release of energy. This regenerative procedure will ensure that our body's old cells continuously break down, as new cells are continuously produced. Physiologists estimate that a man's cells are in continuous transformation, a transformation which lasts for seven years, after which time his entire body has been changed into another body. We look in the mirror and find that our faces change between childhood and adolescence, then from adolescence to middle age, until old age, when we can see that our face is totally different. This proves that regeneration is continuously changing our body in an undetectable way, yet we cannot sense this happening. How stupid we really are!

Meditation can make our central nervous system calm down, so that it can develop its potential, to let the blood's circulation function better, to let the breathing system receive its adjustments, and to help the regenerative processes. The effectiveness of meditation practice on these processes is impressive.

CHAPTER THREE

How to Meditate

What Adjustments to Make Before and After Meditation

Adjusting your diet

The human body is like a machine. A machine requires fuel to operate just as the human body requires food. After being chewed in the mouth, food is blended with saliva, then digested by the liquids in the stomach and turned into a pasty substance which flows into the small intestine for use by the whole body. We know that food plays a very important part in life. However, if too much food is taken in, the stomach cannot fully digest and absorb it; on the contrary, the undigested waste will be expelled from the body. This will increase the stomach's work. Our bodies will be overburdened, and we will become anxious. In this condition we cannot achieve peace in meditation.

If too little food is consumed, we will suffer from malnutrition and physical weakness. This is not appropriate for meditation either. Therefore, we should regulate our food intake. People always like to eat a lot. This is very inappropriate. We should consume food only until we feel somewhat, but not entirely, satiated. There is an old saying that the body should constantly labor, and food should constantly be regulated. This saying I agree with entirely. We should also not require food with a rich flavor. Vegetables are actually more suitable for our body than meat. It is not good to meditate immediately after eating. We should wait about two hours. The most appropriate time for meditation is in the morning after waking, washing one's face, drinking some water, and emptying the bowels.

Adjusting your sleep

After exerting yourself physically and mentally you need to rest in order to renew your energy. We can regard sleep as the longest period we have to really rest. An ordinary person should sleep for eight hours. Exceeding this will make our spirit lose clarity, which is inappropriate for meditation. With too little sleep, our body cannot recover its energy, and our mind stays in a trance-like state. This also is inappropriate for meditation.

Therefore, sleeping should be fixed at a regular time in order to keep our spirit always clear. This creates the best condition for meditation. We can practice meditation sitting on a bed, before going to sleep in the evening, or wake up at midnight to sit in meditation. After meditation, if we feel the need, we can go back to sleep. In any case, time spent sleeping should neither be too much nor too little.

Adjusting your body

Adjusting your body implies adjusting your posture. We should adjust our bodies before, after, and during meditation. Our physical activities include walking, relaxing, sitting, and lying—four postures. The meditation practitioner should be aware of his behavior at all times. His physical behavior should be easy and calm; violent movement is inappropriate. When you behave violently, your energy flow becomes violent, too, and your mind cannot focus on meditation. Therefore, before meditation adjust the mind. This is another method of adjusting the body.

When you enter into meditation on a bed or on a specially made cushion, loosen your belt, and arrange your feet in the right position. Fold both your knees, put your left foot on the right thigh, level with the thigh, then put the right foot on the left thigh. In this posture, the soles face upward, the thighs seem to form a triangle, the two knees press tightly against the bed or cushion, and all the body's muscles are like a fully stretched bow. This is the best posture for meditation, for the practitioner will not lean forward, backward, left or right. However, older persons might have trouble using this posture. They can use a half-folded (single fold) posture—putting only the left foot on the right thigh, no need to put the right foot on the left thigh. Some persons might even have problems with the single fold posture; these persons may sit simply with the legs crossed, one foot touching the opposite thigh. The two hands should be in the right position—both hands open, facing up, with the right hand in the left palm, near the abdomen, resting gently on the legs. Then twist the torso in both directions, left and right, to be certain the posture is well adjusted and stable. The spinal column should not be too stiffly erect, nor too bent. Keep the head erect, so that the nose and the navel are vertically aligned.

At this point open your mouth and exhale the stale air from the chest, curling your tongue back extending towards the throat, with the under surface of the tongue in contact with the palate. Next, one should inhale clean air gently three to seven times through the nose. Then the mouth should be closed, with the tongue in the retroflex position, eyes closed and posture straight and motionless. If you feel the body leaning in any direction, adjust your body to correct this. This is how to adjust your body during meditation.

After meditation (to be described later), open the mouth and breathe out at least ten more times in order to reduce the body temperature. Slowly twist the torso in both directions, lift, then shrug the shoulders, and rotate the head in a circular motion. Then slowly and gently unfold the crossed feet and legs. After this, rub the inner edges of the hands against each other, at the lower part of the thumbs, until they become warm. Before opening the eyes, use these warm parts of the hand to wipe the two eyelids. The back of the thumbs should be used again to rub the two sides of the nose simultaneously. After this, rub the two palms together until they become warm, then, with the two warm palms, rub the back of the ears and the head, chest and abdomen, arms, legs, and both sides of the feet. During meditation the blood circulates more actively, making the body perspire, so wait until the perspiration dries before beginning your regular schedule. This is how to adjust the body after meditation.

Adjusting the breath

Air enters and exits through the nostrils as inhalation and exhalation. One inhalation with one exhalation counts as a single breath. The most essential task for meditation is to adjust that breath. There are four different breathing techniques. The first of these is to breathe with the throat. Ordinary people do not realize that breathing is part of the art of maintaining good health; their breathing is short and shallow. They just let air enter and exit from the short portion of their throats. In this kind of breathing, the lobes of the lungs cannot fully expand and contract. Therefore they cannot fully inhale oxygen and exhale carbon dioxide. This prevents the circulation of blood in the lungs from reaching ideal levels.

The second technique is chest breathing. This technique should be better than the first one, since air reaches the chest and the lobes of the lungs fill with air. When we exercise, we use this technique naturally. However, neither of these techniques qualify as breathing adjustments.

The third breathing technique uses the abdomen. This technique allows you to send the breath all the way to the abdomen. When the practitioner uses this technique to inhale, the air is drawn into and fills his lungs. His lungs are expanded and the diaphragm presses down. At this point, the chest is empty and relaxed, and the stomach expands. When the practitioner exhales, the abdomen contracts and the diaphragm raises up against the lungs, so that the stale air in the lungs is fully expelled from the body. This method may be considered a breathing adjustment. Breathing should not take too much effort. Make the breathing slow and prolonged, both as it enters and exits the body. The air should reach the abdomen in a very natural way, noiselessly, so that you cannot hear the breath as it enters or exits the body. This can be considered an advanced breathing adjustment.

The fourth method is to breathe with the whole body. After several years of meditation, the practitioner achieves breathing which he cannot perceive in any way. Reaching this high level of skill, the practitioner appears to others to be in a state of non-breathing, because the rhythm and the volume of his breathing are so reduced. Though advanced practitioners obviously still have their lungs, they seem to ignore their use. Air seems to go in and out though the pores of their skin. A person who can attain such a level has reached the highest extreme of attainment in breathing adjustment.

Pay careful attention to the breath going in and out through the nostrils. Do not inhale sharply, for this is shallow breathing. Learn to extend the breath from the throat to the chest and to the abdomen. This is the breathing adjustment to use before meditation. During meditation, if the breath is not adjusted, your mind will be unstable. Therefore, adjust the breath to a slow and gentle pace, balancing the duration of the inhalations and exhalations to make them equal. Regulate the breath by counting, either counting the number of exhalations or the number of inhalations. Count first from one to ten, and repeat this count. If your concentration fails during the first ten breaths counted, then start again at one. Continue this practice for quite some time, for it helps develop your skills, and adjusts the breathing correctly. This is part of the method for breathing adjustment during meditation. Breathing adjustment influences the circulatory system, making the blood flow more actively and warming the body. Therefore, after meditation, open the mouth and release the breath to lower the body temperature and re-establish normal body temperature.

At this point, you may resume your activities. This applies to the method for breathing adjustment after meditation.

Adjusting the mind

Right from birth, people seem to enjoy the mind's random thinking. As each random thought dies another arises to take its place. We can describe it this way: "Just as the will gallops like a horse, so the mind acts like a monkey." We can see that the mind is very difficult to adjust. The final result of meditation depends totally on how well you adjust random thoughts. Of the four postures, sitting, lying, walking, and relaxing, we should occasionally check our walking and relaxing. All verbal and physical behavior should be monitored. We should always put our mind inside our bodies; do not let it gallop at random. With prolonged training, it will be easier to adjust the mind. This is how to adjust the mind before meditation.

During meditation, there are two types of problem. The first is that the mind may lose concentration, and not be able to complete the meditation process. The second is that the mind becomes drowsy, and easily drifts towards sleep. The beginning practitioner may easily encounter the problem of losing concentration. After a long period of practice, he will be able to diminish the frequency of random thoughts. Then he risks the problem of getting drowsy. These two are the most frequent problems faced in meditation.

The way to cure the problem of losing concentration is to relinquish all anxieties and look at the physical body as something external to yourself, without thinking about your existence. Focus your mind on the lower abdomen, and gradually you can experience profound tranquility.

The way to cure the problem of drowsiness is to focus your mind on the tip of the nose. Then you can raise your spirit. In my experience, it is easy to become drowsy during evening meditation after working hard during the day. In morning meditation you would not have this problem.

I am recommending some techniques to choose from. The first of these is accurately counting from one to ten. After extensive practice, your mind will follow the breath. With this technique alone, the two problems of losing concentration and of drowsiness may be cured. This is how to adjust the mind during meditation. After meditation, pay attention and do not indulge in random thinking. This is how to adjust the mind after meditation.

I have now described the three ways to adjust the body, breath, and mind. All three should be used simultaneously. I made three separate sections for discussion so that each could be presented clearly, but don't separate these procedures.

CHAPTER FOUR

The Principle of Zhi Kuan

DURING MEDITATION, ARRANGE the torso and four limbs as well as possible, and adjust the breath. The mind is the most difficult to tame. The human mind always likes to chase after external things. Although you would like to recall your errant mind back to the body, this is not an easy task to accomplish, so we must learn and practice the principles of Zhi Kuan, which will allow us to meet this goal. After practicing the three adjustments, learn the principles of Zhi Kuan. Even if you have never heard of the way of adjustment, you can still study the principles of Zhi Kuan.

Zhi means "rest." We have to stop our random thinking. Random thinking is like a monkey which knows no moment of stillness or peace. If this is so, what steps can we take to stop it? If we want the monkey to stop its activity, we have to tie it to a wooden stake, so that he can no longer jump at random. The first step towards practicing Zhi is called Xi Yuan Zhi (determination through tying up attractions). The mind's random activity must be occupied with a specific subject, either concept or object. This attractive subject is called Yuan (the fatal connection, the attractive). The mind thinks randomly first of a, then of b, then of c and d. This is called Pan Yuan (being hooked by the attractive). We tie our minds to some spot, as we might tie up a monkey, so that our mind will not be attracted by anything else, a process we call "achieving rest by tying up the attractive."

There are several ways to cure the mind's problems. I will illustrate two of these to choose from. The first method is to tie the mind to the tip of the nose—free of any random thoughts, focus the mind's eye on the tip of the nose to watch the breath. When you watch the entry and exit of the breath, you see neither where the breath comes from nor where it returns. After extensive practice, your random thoughts will gradually subside.

The second method is to tie the mind to the bottom of the abdomen: the center of gravity of our body is in the lower abdomen, so tying our minds to this place gives us perfect balance. When we do this, we should imagine a straight line from the nose and throat to the abdomen, entering and exiting through our nostrils. After prolonged practice, our mind's random thinking may diminish. This practice can also help in adjusting the breath.

When we have learned to rest by tying up the attractive, we can move on to Zhi Xin Zhi "achieving rest by controlling the mind." What is Zhi Xin Zhi? Xi Yuan deals with the mind's subjectivity. Now Zhi Xin Zhi can directly deal with the mind itself, allowing us to control and stop thought when we discern it in our mind, and prevent the possibilities of being hooked by the attractive. This training is far deeper and far more subtle than that about Xi Yuan Zhi.

As the next step, we learn Ti Zhen Zhi ("resting by understanding the truth"). This practice is on a level even higher than Zhi Xin Zhi. The two methods just described are preparatory steps for learning to rest. When you practice this method you will acquire true rest.

What is Ti Zhen Zhi? Ti means "understanding"; Zhen means "truth." When you try to discern your thoughts they suddenly disperse, become empty and random, and lose all value. If we don't try to perceive our thoughts, the mind remains in a state of void. If in addition all random thinking and conflict are not intentionally controlled, the mind may achieve a state of rest in a natural way. When you dispel empty, random thoughts the mind is close to truth. In this state the mind truly knows rest.

When you practice Ti Zhen Zhi during meditation, close the eyes, and reflect on the memory of your physical growth. We grow from infancy to childhood, maturity, old age, and death. Our cells constantly regenerate, without a moment's pause. There is no physical or mental state to which I can permanently hold and claim as my body. Again we reflect on the mind's thoughts. Thought after thought passes through our minds. The most recent of these is just past, the present thought continues, and the future thought is imminent. Which of these thoughts may I consider to be my true thought? From this we can see that as random mind perishes it is reborn, and all is empty and random. After much practice, we can stop this process of random thought naturally so that the mind remains in a state of truth.

As we learn meditation, our mind easily loses concentration in the beginning stages. This loss of concentration allows the mind to drift. The way to prevent the mind from losing concentration is to learn the technique of achieving rest. Repeated practice teaches our mind to remain in a state of rest. When rest is achieved, we easily become inattentive and drift into sleep. Curing this drowsiness requires visualization. Visualization doesn't mean looking outward, but rather closing the eyes and looking inward, to the mind.

There are three types of visualization. One is called visualizing the void. In this method, we try to visualize all things in the universe as constantly undergoing change, whether they be as large as mountains and rivers, or as small as our bodies and minds. Everything is impermanent. We must look into our minds and visualize this. This is called visualization of the void.

After long years of this practice, you can look into your mind during meditation and find that every thought in the mind has a subject, either an idea or an event. All things in the world result from the interactions of original conditions and ensuing events. For example, the seeds of various grains can sprout. This is an original condition. Water and soil can nourish these seeds. These are the ensuing events, the catalysts. If we store these seeds in a barn, and do not sow them, they would never sprout. Thus there is original condition lacking a catalyst. All things in the world are produced by the meeting of original conditions with a catalyst, and perish by their separation.

Our thoughts are chimerical. Do not try to hang on to them. If we visualize the attainment of goals, we are visualizing an illusion. Relatively speaking, visualization of the void belongs to the realm of non-being, and visualizing illusion belongs to the realm of being. Despite extensive study of visualization, we have not achieved perfection. We should therefore continue our study. When we visualize the void, we should be free from any prejudice that the vision must be void. If we visualize illusion, we create the illusory. Don't become attached to the concepts of void and illusion. Let your mind rely on nothing. If we achieve this, our minds become like hollow caves from which we can witness the external light. This is called visualizing the middle.

Superficially it appears that we are making distinctions in our discussion of this Zhi Kuan principle. In actual practice the practitioner can use his mind freely. Sometimes he may prefer to use resting, sometimes he may prefer to use visualization. Be determined in unifying your thoughts. This is called resting. Directing thoughts is called visualization. When we practice resting, we never abandon the use of visualization. When we practice visualization, we do not abandon the use of resting. Feel free to use both methods, and don't let yourself get confused by their apparent contradictions.

CHAPTER FIVE

The Six Mystical Steps

In Chapter Three, we discussed adjustment. Though we tried to present the three adjustments of the breath, body, and mind equally, this introduction gave preferential treatment to the adjustment of the body. In Chapter Four, we discussed the principle of Zhi Kuan, which is primarily a discussion of the mind. In this chapter, The Six Mystical Steps, emphasis is on the breath.

Breath is the origin of life. Anyone who cannot breathe will soon die. Without breath, the nervous system cannot sustain its reflexes and the mind dies. His life is finished. Breath alone makes it possible for us to connect the body and the mind, and maintain life. The entry and exit of air through our nostrils depends on this breath. Although it is usually invisible to our eyes, breath has both form and weight. Since it has both weight and form, during its passage it is also a material part of our body. We realize that entry and exit of the breath depend entirely on our mind, and that it is part of the spirit. Since breath can connect the body and the mind, we know breath itself is part of the body and the mind.

The Six Mystical Steps will teach the practitioner to manage the technique of breathing. It is a method of continuous meditation. After learning the principles of

Zhi Kuan, the practitioner can go further to study the Six Mystical Steps. Even without practicing the principles of Zhi Kuan, he may begin the study of the Six Mystical Steps.

Step One:
Counting Practice and Fulfillment

The Six Mystical Steps are: Counting, Following, Resting, Visualization, Returning, and Clarifying. What is Counting? Counting is to count breaths. Counting breaths has two levels. The first of these is Counting Practice. After entering meditation, try to adjust the breath so it becomes perfectly smooth and peaceful, then count slowly from one to ten, placing the count on either the inhalation or the exhalation. When you focus on Counting, do not lose concentration. If you lose concentration before ten is reached, begin the process over, starting at one. This is called Counting Practice.

The second level of counting breaths is called Counting Fulfillment. After much practice, you become gradually skillfull enough to count from one to ten without confusion. Your inhalations and exhalations become gentle and soft. When you reach this point, your breathing is so regular that you no longer need to count. This state is called Counting Fulfillment.

Step Two:
Relaxing-mind Practice and Fulfillment

After this, we should give up the practice of Counting, and proceed to study the Relaxing and Following technique. This technique also has two levels, the first of which is called the Relaxing and Following-mind Practice. We give up Counting and let our mind follow the entry and exit of the breath. The mind accompanies the breath and the breath accompanies the mind, closely linked to each other, the breath becoming gentle and soft. This is called Following Practice. The second level of this practice is called Following Fulfillment. Once you master the Relaxing and Following technique, the breath becomes very gentle, and it feels like you could breathe simply through your skin. The mind is placid and still. This state is called Following Fulfillment.

If, after a long period of practice, you feel that the breath is not yet gentle enough, give up the practice of Relaxing and Following-mind and begin the practice of Resting.

Step Three:
Resting Practice and Fulfillment

Resting also has two levels. The first one is called Resting Practice. The mind no longer follows the breath. Now gently focus your mind on the tip of the nose. This is called Resting Practice. After a long period of practice, you will no longer feel that you have a mind or a physical body, and will enter into a state of deep meditation. This is called Resting Fulfillment. Having reached this level of deep meditation, continue to visualize light in your mind until it becomes bright. Don't rest on your laurels, but begin the study of Visualization.

Step Four:
Visualization Practice and Fulfillment

Visualization also has two levels. The first of these to realize is the Visualization Practice. In meditation carefully visualize the breath entering and exiting the body, like a breeze in the air that lacks physical substance.

This is called Visualization Practice. After a long period practicing Visualization, you can mentally watch the breath entering and exiting through every pore in your body. This is called the Embodiment of Visualization and its Fulfillment. In the previous chapter, we discussed resting and visualization. These terms have a different meaning in this chapter. In the previous chapter, we used resting and visualization to focus on training the mind. In this chapter the focus is on training the breath. After practicing Visualization for some time, devote the next period of study to visualize the Returning Practice.

Step Five:
Returning Practice and Fulfillment

Returning, like the other techniques, has two levels. The first of these is to realize the Returning Practice. Once you have used your mind to visualize the breath, the mind acquires the skill of intelligent Visualization. This skill is distinct from intellectual activity, but this opposition is relative, not absolute. The practitioner lets his mind trace the origin of his thoughts. This is called the originality of Returning Practice.

The second level is to verify the Returning Practice, which is called Returning and its Fulfillment. This intelligent Visualization arises from the mind. Since it has arisen within the mind, it should fall within the mind, too. One rising, one falling. These are elusive and unreal. The rising and falling of the mind is like ripples on water. Ripples are not the water itself. We have to wait until the surface of the water is smooth before we can see the water itself. The rising and falling of the mind is like a ripple, which is not truly mind.

We should visualize our true mind, where nothing arises. If nothing arises, then it is non-being. Non-being then becomes the void. If it is the void, then there is no visualizing mind. If there is no visualizing mind, then there is no state for Visualization, and both state and intellectual activity disappear. This is called Returning Fulfillment. Once you have reached the level of Returning Fulfillment, your mind retains only the concept of returning. Go on to the practice of Clarification.

Step Six:
Clarification Practice and Fulfillment

Clarification has two levels also, the first called the emptiness of the Clarification Practice. When the mind is clarified, there will be no thoughts to distinguish. The second level is Clarification Fulfillment, in which the mind stays as still as still water, all random thinking expelled. You can then perceive your true mind. This doesn't mean there is both a true mind and a random-thinking mind. The mind returns from random thinking, and attains truth. This is like a ripple disappearing into the surface of water.

In summing up the principles of the Six Mystical Steps, Counting and Following comprise the preparatory work to use for deep meditation. Resting and Visualization are for prolonged meditation. Returning and Clarification are the fruit of this meditation. In these Six Mystical Steps, Resting should be regarded as the main training, with Visualization simply an aid to enhance the Resting Practice. Then the mind can be clearly disciplined, and you can receive the fruits of meditation, which are the Returning and Clarification.

PART II

CHAPTER SIX

My Experience

My childhood

In my childhood I was a small, weak, and sickly boy. I felt dizzy, sweated at night, and had sores on my genitals. In my sleep I suffered from spermatorrhea. I saw spirits and ghosts, sound filled my ears. All these physical problems occurred. Occasionally, leaving my house I could walk only half a mile before my feet would soften and become so weak that I could go no further. When I was fourteen or fifteen years old, my health problems became more numerous and more severe. I felt like I was in a trance, I suffered from floating fears, and felt my body struck by waves of heat. I still remember the spring when I was sixteen; every afternoon my body overheated, then became cool again by the following morning. This condition continued until the summer.

I became very sick with tuberculosis, and called on doctors to diagnose me. They prescribed different medicines, but these never improved my condition. In my home I had a Chinese medical book, *I Fen Chi Kuei* (*General Answers to Medical Questions*), which explained that tuberculosis could not be cured by relying on medicine alone. This book recommends that patients be nursed in quiet surroundings, so that they may recover gradually. The book also introduces the art of Taoist meditation, Xiao Zho Tian (small heaven circulation), and describes in detail how to develop this practice. I followed the instructions and practiced Taoist meditation. What eventually happened to me convinced me of its effectiveness.

I practiced meditation very diligently when I was ill, but when the symptoms disappeared, I stopped practicing. I lacked devotion. Though occasionally I was still ill, my general health was much better than it had been before I began the meditation practice. When I was twenty-one years old, I got married. Thinking my health was quite good, I gave up the practice of meditation. During this time, however, I had sex too frequently, so my old sickness struck me again. I also ate too much, which resulted in severe stomach aches. My esophagus was feverish, and my stomach made noise constantly. Even when I longed for food, if it was presented to me I could not swallow it.

In the spring when I was twenty-six, my elder brother died of tuberculosis, and I was also infected. At twenty-seven years old, my coughing became relentless, and later I spat blood. This condition lasted three months. My health was becoming worse each day. Finally, I decided to throw away all my medicines, give up sex, live alone in a separate room, leave all worldly worries behind, and practice meditation. I forced myself to meditate four times a day, at midnight, six in the morning, noon, and at six in the evening. Each time I meditated for one or two hours. I continued this practice for three months. Eventually I felt my abdomen gradually become warm. This feeling of heat became stronger and stronger, until it circulated and trembled in my abdomen like boiling water. On the evening of May twenty-ninth, I felt a jerky quiver in my abdomen, then a flood of hot air flushed against the base of my spine, and, following the Jia Ji[1] sympathetic nerve, surged up to the base of my brain. The meridian along this line is called the Tu or Governor meridian, in the traditional Chinese medical dictionary. I felt this sensation six times, before it gradually stopped.

I realized then that only eighty-five days had passed since the first day, March fifth, when I had resumed practicing meditation. After this experience, every time I entered into meditation, the heat would follow the same path, reaching the summit, but the quivering never recurred. It seemed that after the quivering experience, I had been switched into another body. Not only were all my old diseases cured, but I could easily walk for more than ten miles without feeling tired.

Since that time I have never discontinued meditation practice. When I was twenty-eight years old, I was hired as a tutor. I simply rearranged my meditation schedule, changing it to twice a day, once in the morning and once in the evening. On the morning of March twenty-eighth of the same year, I felt the heat quivering in my abdomen again. From there it came up my Jia Ji sympathetic nerve, and flushed against the base of my brain. For three days the heat continued. I felt like the bone at the back of my brain had opened, as a tide of heat flowed into the crown of my head. After this experience, this sensation recurred every time I entered into meditation; the heat flowed along the same path, but without quivering.

---

1 Jia Ji Xue (acupuncture points beside the vertebrae) were invented and introduced by Dr. Huo Tou (about 156–214 AD). The 17 points in this group are located 0.5 cun (1 inch) lateral to the spinal column, at the level of the lower border of each spinous process from thoracic vertebra 1 to lumbar vertebra 5. The Jia Ji points from thoracic vertebra 1 to thoracic vertebra 12 are known as thoracic Jia Ji, and those from lumbar vertebra 1 to lumbar vertebra 5 are known as lumbar Jia Ji.

At midnight on October fifth of that year, I felt the quivering in my abdomen again, and the heat circulating at the crown of my head changed direction, rushing down my face, separating into two parts around my nose and mouth, then reuniting at my throat. This flush of heat continued down along the vagus nerve, through my chest, then flowed into my lower abdomen. In traditional Chinese medical terms, this path is called the Jen or Conceptional meridian.

After this experience, every time I entered into meditation, the heat flowed from the spot of my Wei Lu (at the base of the spine), up along my Jia Ji sympathetic nerve, and ascended to the crown of my head. Then it went back down over my face and chest to my abdomen. The heat repeated the established circuit through the Governor and Conceptional meridians. I did not feel the quivering. Since this time, except for a few instances when I took medicine, I have never been ill again. Therefore I believe that my experience has proven that the Taoist art of meditation has a preventive effect against disease.

My adult history

When I was thirty years old, I went to Shanghai to study philosophy, physiology, psychology, and public health. Using this knowledge, I tried to analyze the effects associated with my meditation practice, to increase my understanding of them. This type of training led me to prefer using scientific terms and analysis to describe the theory of meditation. As a result, to illustrate this theory, I gradually gave up using the metaphors of Yin and Yang, the Five Elements, Lead, Mercury, and I Ching's terms such as K'an and Li. I published my first meditation book,

Yin Shi Zi's Meditation, in 1914, when I was forty-one years old.

The year I was forty-two (1915), I went to Beijing for the second time. There I studied Buddhism, and my fellow students persuaded me to learn Buddhist meditation also. At that time, Master Ti-Hsien was preaching in Beijing, giving sermons on the sutra of *Yuean-Ju Ching.* From him, I learned the method of Zhi Kuan, the secret of cultivating Tian Tai Tsung, one of the branches of Buddhism. Some of my fellow students urged me to write another book about my meditation, so I wrote down my thoughts, based on my understanding of Tung Meng Zhi Kuan (a child's resting mind) and the practice of *Po-Lo-Mi-T'o* (*The Diamond Sutra*). This led to the completion of my second meditation book, called *The Continuation of Yin Shi Zi's Meditation.* After this, I concentrated on cultivating the practice of Zhi Kuan.

Studying Eastern Tantra

When I was fifty-three years old, ten or more of my devoted religious friends intended to study the Eighteen Points of Eastern Tantra with Master E Yin Li. At that time, I had not developed sufficient faith in Tantra. My friends urged me insistently to join them, and since I was curious to know more about Tantra, I attended those teachings. I found their ceremonies very ornate and tedious. I did not have adequate time to study Tantra, because I was teaching at Kuan Hua university and my teaching duties were quite extensive. Because of my busy schedule, I was obliged to give up my study of Tantra. I did not, however, discontinue the practice of Zhi Kuan principles.

The changing sensations
of my physical body

In the principles of Tung Meng Zhi Kuan, it says that when one enters into deep meditation, some positive sensations will occur. There are eight of these sensations, which are: lightness, warmth, cold, sinking, pulsating force, itching, dryness, and slipperiness. The first four sensations are without motion; the second four involve motion. Also, in my experience, these sensations do not occur simultaneously. Some come earlier, some later.

When I was around twenty-seven years old, I had the sensations of lightness, warmth, and the pulsating force. My first sensation occurred after a lengthy period of meditation. I felt my whole body become very light, light as a feather. The next sensation was heat in my lower abdomen, and then the pulsating force arose, moving up my spinal nerve to my brain. It crossed to the front of my head, and came down over my face, along the vagus nerve, and reached my lower abdomen. This circulating pattern repeated, with the pulsating force apparently touching my Conceptional and Governor meridians. In the records of traditional Chinese medicine, there are Extraordinary Acupoints and eight other meridians which include the Conceptional and Governor meridians. The first of these meridians is called the Tsung or Impersian meridian. The second is called the Dai or Belt meridian, and the others, the Yang Chiao, the Yin Chiao, the Yang Wei, and the Yin Wei meridians.

For the last ten years I had focused in my meditation exclusively on my lower abdomen. I now shifted the focus to the middle Dan Tien. Within only a few days, I felt an enormous change occur in my body. It seemed that six meridians were affected: the Yang Chiao, Yin Chiao, Yang Wei, Yin Wei, Tsung, and Dai. I will try to describe the circumstances in detail.

The first episode

Once, after I shifted my focus to the middle Dan Tien, I woke up to meditate at midnight. I felt a sudden tremor in my heart and chest, and my mouth filled with saliva. This continued for several evenings. The tremors in my heart became more frequent, and the pulsating force coursed up to the space between my eyebrows, where I intuitively felt that a red light was emitted. The radiance of this light filled the crown of my head, circulating there for a long time. My whole body felt as if an electric field surrounded me, penetrating at the palms of my hands and the bottoms of my feet. It lasted for one minute, then suddenly stopped at my eyebrows.

After that, this happened every evening. It seemed as though there were some device in my middle Dan Tien controlling this circulating current. The current moved up from there to the crown of my head, and my crown turned violently as the current spun around. After this violent turning, the current stopped abruptly between my eyebrows. Then my middle Dan Tien trembled again. It seemed there was an electric field surrounding the area in my upper body from my left shoulder to my left leg, making a slanting circle, and my bed and my mosquito net were shaken by this quivering. After the violence, the quivering came to a stop.

The quivering occurred again at the base of my brain, and the pulsating force flowed down along my spine and lingered at the bottom of my spine at the spot of Wei

Lu. Once again, from my right shoulder to my right leg, I felt the presence of an electric field surrounding the upper half of my body with oblique circles. After violent activity, it abruptly stopped. The current had circulated around my right and left legs and made oblique circles which flushed through the paths of four meridians: the Yin Chiao, Yang Chiao, Yin Wei, and Yang Wei. In my experience, the Extraordinary Acupoints and the eight meridians were consistent with the function of the nervous system. This is true, with no exaggeration.

Every time I meditated and focused on the middle Dan Tien, I felt a change occur. One evening the pulsating force flowed across my face, from one ear to the other. It seemed as if there was a horizontal line being drawn, and this line waved to the left and to the right several times. Without warning, the pulsating force stopped between my eyebrows. Then it started again, surging downwards from the top of my head to my chin, making a vertical line. It crossed the horizontal line it had previously traced, forming a cross. The current went up and down this line several times, then stopped abruptly once more at the midpoint between my brows. Starting up again at my crown, the pulsating force curved downward to my chest, then descended to my sexual organ, making it rise up. Coursing down from my head in this way, the force made my organ quiver several times. I felt this curved line of force was flushing through a path which began at the bottom of my Conceptional meridian and reached the end of the Governor meridian.

The second episode

One evening my middle Dan Tien felt hot, and I felt a surge of the pulsating force. My whole body was bent forward, then backward, to the left, then to the right. I was waved in this same manner several times, each time being pushed forward, backward, left, then right, with no conscious effort on my part. Next, the quivering came up through my hands, moving my hands in a circular motion as fast as a machine. My hands moved in tandem from side to side.

After this, the pulsating force came up through my feet, making first my left foot bend and my right foot straighten, then my right foot bend and my left foot straighten. I could not consciously control this motion, it was totally beyond my physical or logical control. Immediately afterwards this activity in my legs and arms stopped, and I felt my head and my torso swell up to a size of about ten feet. (According to Buddhist sutra, this is the sign of becoming a Buddha—that one has achieved a giant stature.) All at once my head bent backwards and my chest swelled even more, until I felt it was filled with an extensive void. Once again I was bent forward, my back swelled up, and I felt a similar sensation of being filled with a large, void space. At this point I had normal sensation only in my lower body, as if I had no upper torso, and my body and mind were filled with this state of void. This feeling was quite pleasant.

The third episode

Another evening, I felt the pulsating force move from my middle Dan Tien to surround my spine, circulating from left to right, then right to left, equally in both directions. I felt it move under the skin of my back, from left to right, tracing a big circle, dozens of times. This was repeated in the opposite direction, from right to left. Next I felt it circulate in my abdomen, turning from left to right and right to left around my Conceptional meridian. After this, the pulsating force encircled my waist, moving from left to right, forming a big circle, again, dozens of times, as it had in my back. The circle then reversed directions, from right to left, and repeated the same pattern dozens of times. This sequence indicated that my Dai meridian was flushed through.

After this, the pulsating force spiraled downwards in several dozen progressively smaller circles, in a cone shape which followed the path of the Governor meridian from the back of my crown to my Jia Ji acupoint, then down to the Wei Lu. In passing, the pulsating force flushed through my Governor and Conceptional meridians, then ascended from my Wei Lu up my spine to the crown of my head. It then flowed down from the base of my brain to the Jia Ji, and returned to the Wei Lu. This happened dozens of times. Once more, beginning at my lower abdomen, the pulsating force followed the Conceptional meridian, rose up to the crown of my head, flowed down from the base of my brain through the Jia Ji to return again to the Wei Lu. It traced this path dozens of times. In this way the pulsating force completed the circuit which it had begun within me, touching my Conceptional and Governor meridians from the Wei Lu in my back, along the Jia Ji points, up to my crown, my face, then dropping down to my abdomen.

The next time it started, it moved in the opposite direction. I think that because my meridians were unobstructed, the flow was able to follow a natural path within my body—it could flow from the front or from the back, which proved that my Tsung meridian and the Dai meridian were at that point totally unobstructed.

The fourth episode

Another night, I sensed this pulsating force in my middle Dan Tien, and it drew a spiral with a diameter of about two inches on the surface of my skin. This pattern started at the center of my middle Dan Tien and extended out to both sides of my body. This pattern went first to the left, then to the right. Each time it started, the pulsating force traced thirty-six spiral patterns. Afterwards, it moved to my abdomen, and made thirty-six spirals in the same pattern on the skin, first to the left, then to the right. Then the force moved upward, to the skin of my chest, repeating the same circular, spiral motion, first to the left, then to the right, thirty-six times. I had the impression that these three events in my lower body, the center of my body, and my upper body, were pre-arranged in a specific order.

Following this, the force ascended to my crown, and, following a line which spiraled down my spine, it reached my Wei Lu, where it stopped. Then it rose, spiraling around my spine again. In this way it reached my crown, then retracted its path up and down my spine twice. The pulsating force then spiraled up from the left side of my lower abdomen, just left of my Tsung meridian, to my crown, where it started down along the same path. Then it spiraled up from the right side of my lower abdomen, just right of my Tsung meridian, reaching my crown. From my crown, it passed down along the same path.

After this sequence, it encircled my Conceptional meridian, at the level of my head. Next, it passed back down to my lower abdomen, circulated once more, and ascended to my crown. Sometimes it moved in a left to right circular motion in my head, stopping at my forehead. First it circled around my left shoulder, next it circled around my right shoulder, an equal number of times in each direction. Suddenly this pulsating force reached between my fingers, and my fingertips shook with no conscious control. This shaking was very rapid, yet like dancing, for it had a clear and obvious pattern. Just as suddenly the pulsating force passed down from my crown and reached my two feet simultaneously. Both feet were straightened out at this time, and the tips of my toes moved in the same rapid, circular, dancelike pattern as the fingers had moved.

The fifth episode

Another night the pulsating force traced a flat spiral pattern on the skin at the center of my back. Beginning at the center, this moving pattern extended to both sides of my body. First the spiral pattern went towards the left, then to the right, as it had before. Also, just as before, the force traced this pattern exactly thirty-six times. Right after this, the pulsating force created this same spiral pattern with thirty-six repetitions on the skin of my flanks. Next, this pattern was drawn on the skin at the top of my shoulder blades, again with thirty-six repetitions of the spiral. The patterns all seemed to have the same structured form. As I mentioned before, I felt the pulsating force move from the middle Dan Tien down to my lower abdomen, then up to my chest. Each time the motion was circular, from left to right, then right to left, with only three repetitions of the pattern. This motion began again at the center of my back, moved down to my flanks, then arced up around my shoulders and armpits, swirling to the left and to the right, three times in each direction.

All the repetitions of the pattern were symmetrical. This was my physiological activity—so marvelous, yet quite beyond my powers of imagination! Again, the pulsating force started at my crown, and spread out to my fingertips, and the tips of all my toes. All my fingertips and the tips of my toes then seemed to start dancing again, as they moved in patterns with each of my feet and fingers alternately straight, then bent. In rhythm with this straightening and bending of my feet and fingertips, my cheeks rubbed up and down against my shoulders. These movements were quite rapid.

Suddenly the pulsating force reached up to my nose and made my nostrils expand and contract. Next it reached my eyes and made my eyelids open and close in a quivering motion, while my eyeballs rotated in a circular motion. After this, the pulsating force touched the edges of my ears, and my ears moved in a circular pattern that seemed very natural, thirty-six times, from left to right, then right to left.

The sixth episode

Another evening, my middle Dan Tien generated the pulsating force, which began with a repetitive circular movement. It started at my two flanks, then it surrounded my waist at the level known as the Dai meridian. The motion of the pulsating force was circular, it encircled me from left to right, then right to left, thirty-six times.

It moved up to my chest, and made a horizontal circle once, then circled first to the left, then to the right, thirty-six times. Next it dropped down to the lower area of my abdomen, made a circle around it, then moved to the left and right, making thirty-six circles in each direction. This circular motion shifted from the lower to the middle to the upper area of my torso and was repeated three times. Then it traced circles vertically up and down the left side of my chest. Next, it repeated this pattern on the right side of my chest. After this, the circles alternated from left to right, consecutively, several times.

The pulsating force changed location again, touching my hands and feet simultaneously. The feeling of the force caused my hands to open, and both my arms spontaneously made rapid circles through the air, from front to back. Next, the feeling touched my feet, making them bend, then straighten. This movement was beyond my conscious control. Occasionally my feet moved close to each other, and the toes touched, with my heels apart. Following this, my two heels touched, and my feet turned out, pointing away from each other. My knees also alternately touched each other, then separated. Suddenly my knees were raised up, and my hips were suspended in the air, waving from left to right. At the same time, my hands and feet moved three times. Then the pulsating force moved up to my cheeks, my lips, my nose, my eyes, and my ears, just as I have described it previously, but this time it happened faster.

The seventh episode

One evening, I started to feel the circulation in my middle Dan Tien, left and right, as the pulsating force traced a design which extended from my chest to my lower abdomen. Like the ones I described earlier, this pattern was also a spiral, but this time it happened more times, at the middle, lower, and upper parts of my torso. At each location, there were sixty repetitions of the pattern instead of the thirty-six I had previously experienced. Suddenly I felt that the spiral drawn on my middle Dan Tien was expanding. I felt hollow inside. From my chest to my abdomen, this spiraling motion was expanding, and I felt completely hollow. Separately at each of the three levels, upper, middle, and lower, the circles enlarged, approximately six times. Each time a circle was completed, the feeling lasted about five to six minutes.

After that, the pulsating force went up from my middle Dan Tien to my crown, and circulated there. Then it dropped down to my left buttock and my left upper body, and traced an oblong shape around my torso thirty-six times. Once more it ascended to my head, then dropped down again to my right buttock, and right half of my torso, repeating the same oblong pattern, moving up and down thirty-six times. After this, it ascended to my head again, and from the base of my brain it flowed down my spine to my Wei Lu. From there it continued down, and paused in my left leg. It next encircled my left leg, then switched to my right leg, and encircled it, too. It circled each leg thirty-six times.

The eighth episode

One evening, I felt the pulsating force move in my middle Dan Tien, my lower abdomen, and my chest. I felt this force move up to my brain, where within my skull I felt the circling movement of the force, right to left and left to right, thirty times.

From the base of my brain it flowed down along my spine to my Wei Lu. At this moment my two feet bent, then straightened, touched each other, then separated. The force next raised up to my abdomen, then up to my two shoulders and to my hands. It ascended to my crown once more, and from there it passed through my cheeks, down my face to my throat. It affected my left shoulder, then my right shoulder, causing them to move in a circular motion—afterwards the same thing happened to my two hands.

Next it reached my feet, which bent, then straightened, then touched each other, then separated. Suddenly, my body was bent into a triangular shape: the pulsating force pushed me onto the floor, so I was lying on my back, supported by my shoulders and my shins, with my torso suspended.

My hips turned left and right, then my flanks turned, making my whole body move at an angle from left to right, slanting. Next, I lay flat on the ground, with the soles of my feet naturally rubbing against each other, then the sole of my left foot rubbed my right leg and the bottom of my right foot rubbed my left—they both rubbed the same number of times.

The pulsating force moved next up to my shoulders and the palms of my hands rubbed each other lengthwise. Suddenly the pulsating force made my two hands rub my neck, then my cheeks, from my chin to my ears, front to back. I continued to rub these places, then the base of my skull, my eyes, the sides of my nose, my ears, then my arms crossed and I rubbed my two shoulders and my upper arms, my left arm with my right hand, and right arm with my left hand.

Next my two crossed hands rubbed my lower abdomen, my chest, then my shoulders, and my back, first the upper back, then the flanks, the hips, the legs, the tops of my feet, my toes, and my arches. Once again this pulsating force raised up. It bent my two arms, then my hands turned to fists, and I patted my shoulders with my fists. The backs of my hands then patted the sides of my neck, under my chin, and my face, in a circular motion around my eyes and on both sides of my nose, then, also in a circular pattern, around my ears. Next my fists patted my temples, and my two hands crossed to my two shoulders, slowly squeezing them, as if kneading them, and again I drew my hands down and squeezed my upper arms. I squeezed my neck and the skin on my face, pinching it between my fingers. I rubbed my chest, my abdomen, my flanks, my lower back, my hips, my legs, the tops of my feet, and my arches.

I consider this natural massage a physiological phenomenon. The patting and squeezing was orderly and always balanced in number; it seemed well organized. I think I could never consciously guide myself through this sequence—it was just marvelous!

After this, parts of the sequence I have just described happened every evening. Sometimes one part of the sequence would repeat for more than ten days, sometimes several parts of the sequence would occur in a single evening. This continued for half a year before it gradually diminished, then stopped, and did not recur. After those six months, I did not feel the pulsating force again in the middle Dan Tien. This is probably because there was no obstruction in any of my meridians, so I no longer felt any kind of pulsating force.

Here is a summary and classification of all these movement types. There were four kinds: hands waving and feet dancing, tapping, rubbing, and squeezing.

CHAPTER SEVEN

My Study and Practice of Tibetan Mahamudra

Learning the secrets of Tibetan Tantra: opening the crown of the head

This Tibetan Tantric secret—allowing you to be reborn into the Buddha's Pure Land—has never been taught in the Han nation of China. This doctrine teaches that on his deathbed a man can visualize his rebirth in the Pure Land, allowing his consciousness to leave his body through the crown of his head. With this goal in mind, the aspirant learns to recite a secret mantra. Once the aspirant receives the experience of opening his crown, and practices this process frequently, he will be able to follow a defined path at the time of his death. In 1933 I was sixty years old. I learned this secret from Master No Na. At the time he showed me the secret, he wanted me to practice at home. Despite my practice, however, I didn't experience the desired effects.

In the spring of 1937, when I was sixty-four years old, I heard that Master Sheng Lu was teaching this secret in Nanking. Four sessions had already been taught. It was said that every participant could open his crown during the session. When the fifth session was about to start, I thought I shouldn't miss this opportunity, so I hurried to

Nanking. I reached P'i Lo temple in Nanking that same day, and enrolled in the class for opening the crown (which is called Po Wa—breaking the tile, breaking the crown).

On April 1, I arrived at P'i Lo temple, and received the empowerment called Pouring the Blessing Through the Opening of the Crown. This ceremony was much more complicated than Master No Na's. The Master taught us to recite the Ho Mu Chin Kang mantra to facilitate the process. Although the mantra was not long, the method of visualization was quite tedious and complicated, and we had to recite the mantra a hundred thousand times. However, we didn't have much time and the requested number of repetitions was impossible to complete in the space of only a few days, so all of us recited the mantra as many times as possible before receiving the empowerment.

Beginning on the second day, I stayed in my lodgings, shut the door and didn't go out. I concentrated on reciting this mantra until the morning of the last day, by which time I had recited the mantra sixty-two thousand times. In the afternoon of this same day, I changed my lodging to the P'i Lo temple. There were thirty-nine other participants in this training. It was said that this session had more participants than the previous sessions. The Master had us shave a small circular area of hair at our crowns, so that he could examine it during the process of opening the crown. Accordingly, he prepared some lucky reeds, which were to be inserted in the opening which would occur in the shaved, circular area of our crowns.

On the tenth day the temple gate was closed. An ornate altar was set up in the temple's imposing hall. The hall was exquisitely decorated. The Master called us before the altar to receive the empowerment. Every day there were four classes, each of which lasted for two hours: the first class lasted from seven to nine in the morning, the second class, from ten to twelve, the third, from three to five in the afternoon, and the fourth, from seven to nine in the evening. The empowerment procedure involved visualizing the Patron Buddha sitting at the top of one's head. From my crown to my pelvis, there was a tunnel which was blue colored on the outside and red on the inside, and my lower Dan Tien had a shining pearl which rose from there to my heart. Then I shouted "Hey," with effort, and visualized this pearl rising rapidly with this sound, dashing out through my crown to the heart of the Patron Buddha. Then again I called out, not quite so loud, "Gha" and visualized the pearl returning through my crown from the heart of the Buddha, and dropping back down to its place of origin in my lower Dan Tien. Every session everyone shouted so loudly that they became hoarse and perspired so heavily that their clothes were wet all the way through. (At this time it was still cold, and everybody was wearing thin cotton jackets.) The Master saw that most of us were tired, so he sang a Sanskrit song and wanted us to sing in unison with him so that we could be refreshed by singing. During these two hours, we had four or five rest periods.

Owing to my meditation practice I had an unobstructed central channel running from my pubic region to my crown, and I was able to feel wonderful effects on the eleventh day. In the first class, my crown emitted red light, and my size increased to a great stature. In the fourth class, I felt as if there was a force drilling against my crown, and the pearl was dashing up constantly. When I lay down I felt that my head was emitting white light.

On the twelfth day, I practiced as I had the previous day, and in the second class I felt my skull was splitting at my crown. The two bones covering this spot were separating. In the third class, my head swelled up and a lump appeared at my crown. It seemed as though my scalp would split.

In the first class on the thirteenth day, I felt that every layer of my brain had been pierced. At first, I felt that my skull was quite thick, then the drilling made it become thin. In the third class, I suddenly felt my upper body to be in a void state, and my head emitted light. The light's luminosity was increasing. In the first and second classes of the fourteenth day, the pearl was shooting up to the feet of the Patron Buddha, and I felt this route was smooth and unobstructed. The splitting felt quite different in nature from the previous day. Because of the change in sensation on the previous day, I thought that the route was still in some way obstructed. In the first class, I felt my neck was a freely flowing column which led directly to my stomach and my intestines. Prior to this, I had thought that my central channel was opened and unobstructed, which was only my imagination, since it was now proven to be true.

In the first class of the fifteenth day, I felt there was a cavity at my crown. In the second class, the Master ordered us to move closer to the window, where the sunshine was brighter. Next he called each one of us to come up so that he could perform the ritual that would make the crowns open, and then insert a lucky reed into this opening as a token of remembrance. If a practitioner's crown was actually opened, the grass would be sucked in and the scalp would seal up around it. I was among those who had reached this level of attainment. The first time there were twenty-eight persons whose crowns were opened. For the other eleven persons the grass could not be inserted, which indicated they needed to receive more instruction. All of us whose crown had been opened would not continue the practice of this ritual. However, we came up to the altar and used the power of visualization to help those who hadn't had their crowns opened, to help facilitate their attainment in the procedure of opening the crown.

On the sixteenth day, all of us who had their crowns opened came up again to the altar to help. In the first class, another nine persons' crowns were opened. The last group included a nun and a Buddhist woman who could not have their crowns opened. This nun had practiced secret Tantric arts in Japan. Her attainment was quite profound, yet she had great difficulty in making her crown open. A person shouldn't be overconfident, and should always receive teachings with humility. Otherwise, your goal can be difficult to attain. As for this Buddhist woman, I thought she was old and lacked intelligence. The Master called those in the last group to come in front of his cushion, and then personally empowered them. About an hour later, with the assistance of all of us who had their crowns opened, she had her crown opened.

Afterwards I primarily practiced meditation using the principle of Zhi Kuan, and I practiced Po Wa (opening the crown). On the twenty-fourth of May I entered into meditation and felt quiet surround me. My chest emitted light which gradually increased and surrounded my whole body, until the light became a large circle. Previously, I had felt light emit from my head, but this was the first time had felt light emit from my chest region. However, I was still conscious of my existence and my whole body was not totally transparent.

On the twenty-sixth day, when I entered into meditation and became quiet, I felt my back emit light, and my whole body was surrounded by brightness, which gave me a very pleasant feeling, but I still felt I had a body which was not in a void state.

On the twenty-seventh day, when I entered into meditation and became quiet, I emitted very bright light which shot up into the clouds and my soul parted from me. Later I gradually drew it back through my crown.

On the thirty-first day of the same month, after I entered into meditation, my upper body emitted light just as it had the day before. I felt my lower abdomen was boiling like water. My lower body was in a void state, also emitting light, which had never occurred before.

On the tenth of June, after I entered into meditation my whole body emitted a very bright light and I felt as if I had no head. There appeared only a transparent light.

On the fourteenth of June, after I entered into meditation my whole body emitted light. Both my upper and lower body were shining with a transparent light.

On the seventeenth day of June, after I entered into meditation, my whole body emitted light, and felt it illuminate my mind and eyes. This was so bright that my entire body, top, bottom, and sides, was surrounded with a light which expanded into a large circular shape.

On the eighteenth day, after I entered into meditation, my whole body emitted light, and this light was even brighter. My entire body was surrounded with bright transparent light. The light seemed like a single guided burst, directed to the four corners. My consciousness was travelling through the air. Then I withdrew it and returned to my lower abdomen, and as I continued with this practice, my consciousness went down to my feet, up to my two hands, and back to my head.

About the practice of Tibetan Mahamudra

In 1947, when I was seventy-four years old, I followed Master Gonga to learn Mahamudra. In the esoteric school of Sutrayana, the most popular sects are Pure Land and Zen. The Pure Land sect claims that your karma follows you into rebirth. The Zen sect emphasizes the process of training the mind to be tranquil in order to attain wisdom, to eventually attain Buddhahood. Tibetan Tantra's secret of opening the crown demonstrates a way to rebirth in the Pure Land and Mahamudra has the Zen school's characteristic of tranquility. However, I found the methods of Mahamudra practice more practical and workable than those of Zen and Pure Lands, so from that time on I have continued the Mahamudra practice. Maybe someone would ask me, "I know that you have studied Buddhism, first you study the Sutrayana, and then you study the Vajrayana—this is quite contrary to the proper attitude towards acquiring knowledge, don't you think your knowledge is too impure? How can you actually achieve your goal?" I would answer, "It is not so. Though I have studied different schools, I have never abandoned the practice of striving for tranquility, and all these schools are just helping me to make progress towards attaining tranquility."

When you learn the secret of Po Wa (opening the crown), you can have the promise of rebirth. When you learn Mahamudra, your practice of tranquil abiding can grow from a shallow state to a profound state. When people thought I was confused in my knowledge, actually my learning followed a straight line, and perseveres.

These two methods, Mahamudra and the Po Wa, which form the experience I have cultivated and practiced, are very popular in the province of Sekong and in Tibet. They do, however, require personal instruction by a lama.

This practice should not be undertaken alone. Readers, please pay attention to this warning.

Conclusion of My Experience

THE RELATIONSHIP BETWEEN THEORY AND PRACTICE

IN THIS WORK I gave a theoretical presentation of essential principles, and described the methods I practiced myself. My experiences are a testament to the methods' results. When theory and experience unite, effects will naturally be produced. If you study a body of knowledge, or devote yourself to cultivation, you are making a big mistake if you only pursue theory, and don't pay attention to practice. No matter how profound your achievement in theoretical learning, if you do not go on practicing, all this theory is like building a house on the beach—the foundation is not stable.

As the saying goes, "Just talking about food will not make you full." If someone tells you which is the tastiest food, the most delicious, but you haven't eaten it yet, how can you become full? There is another type of person who is afraid that the theory might be too profound and too difficult to understand, so they cast aside the theory and concentrate on practicing. However, practice without method is blind practice. Not only may you fail to benefit from the practice, but you may actually encounter serious pitfalls. This illustrates the problems of abandoning theory. The relationship between theory and practice should be like the wheel and axle of the cart, neither of which can move if the other is neglected.

Traditional Chinese meditation has recently attracted the world's attention, and its development has been rapid. There are many cases of chronic disease being healed through traditional Chinese meditation. The ancient and most popular art of acupuncture is once again being promoted. Though the arts of acupressure and massage may not enjoy as much fame as acupuncture, their theoretical application is nonetheless quite similar. Both serve as healing methods for disease. Of these, only meditation can serve as preventive medical care, which has been passed down through generations. Though it has been neglected for several centuries, the world is now paying attention, and this must be considered good news.

Meditation develops your innate energies. With practice, you can take charge of your mind and body, preventing disease before it arises. Shouldn't everyone make an effort to learn something like this? Superficially, meditation looks easy, but if you practice without patience, determination, and a long-term sense of devotion you will never realize its benefits. Therefore, to give readers a guide to meditation, I have summarized my many decades of experience. As for further explanation, this still awaits the study and research of future scholars of physiology and medicine. This study should help to further promote the role of traditional Chinese meditation in influencing and benefiting the whole world. This is my wish.

Finished in October, 1954

ABOUT THE TRANSLATORS

SHIFU HWANG IS a practicing Taoist from Chuen Zen School. Currently, he lives in Texas, USA. Master Hwang has devoted his adult life to promoting Taoism and balanced health care. In 1996, he established TaiChi People Herb Co. Recently, he established Immortal Cancer Care Foundation for alternative cancer care education.

CHENEY CROW GREW up in Washington, D.C. and graduated from Sarah Lawrence College in New York. She lived and worked in England, France and Spain for several years before completing her Ph.D. in Linguistics, then teaching at the University of Texas at Austin. She studied Long Form Yang Style and Sword Form Tai Chi with Shifu Hwang.

INDEX

Z